WARRIOR SCIENCE

NINJA Science

Camouflage, Weapons and Stealthy Attacks

by Marcia Amidon Lusted

a Capstone company — publishers for children

Raintree is an imprint of Capstone Global Library Limited, a company incorporated in England and Wales having its registered office at 264 Banbury Road, Oxford, OX2 7DY – Registered company number: 6695582

www.raintree.co.uk
myorders@raintree.co.uk

Edited by Aaron Sautter
Designed by Steve Mead
Picture research by Pam Mitsakos
Production by Steve Walker
Originated by Capstone Global Library Limited
Printed and bound in China

Capstone Press would like to thank Michael Wert, PhD, of Marquette University, Wisconsin for his assistance in creating this book.

ISBN 978 1 474 71122 7
20 19 18 17 16
10 9 8 7 6 5 4 3 2 1

British Library Cataloguing in Publication Data
A full catalogue record for this book is available from the British Library.

Acknowledgements
Bridgeman Images: Katsushika Hokusai/Pictures from History, 19, Tomioka Eisen/Pictures from History, 11, Toyohara Chikanobu /Pictures from History, 26, Toyokuni Kunisada/Pictures from History, 4–5, Utagawa Kunikazu/Pictures from History, 25, Utagawa Kunisada/Pictures from History, 20; Shutterstock: Akura Yochi, top cover background, design element throughout book, Anna Jurkovska, cover bottom right, burnel1, cover right, 13 middle left, Chanclos, 9, chrisbrignell, 15, dotshock, 23, Eky Studio, cover, design element throughout book, Fotokvadrat, 12, 28, Guayo Fuentes, 16, Ienjoyeverytime, 22 right, Ijansempoi, 8, KPG Payless2, backcover, cover left, 7, 13 right, 22 left, MyImages – Micha, 14, cover top middle, prochasson Frederic, cover bottom middle, Przemek Tokar, 29, zig8, cover bottom left: Wikimedia/Samuraiantiqueworld, 10

CONTENTS

SHADOWY WARRIORS

A shadowy figure sneaks through the night somewhere in medieval Japan. An enemy's fortress looms above, guarded and impossible to enter. But the man dressed in black has followed a servant to the castle. He kills the servant and puts on his victim's armour. Then he enters the castle in disguise. Soon the fortress gates swing open. Dozens of other ninjas swarm inside and take over the fortress.

Ninja warriors sometimes served a *daimyo*, or lord. They worked mostly in the shadows as spies, **assassins** and **saboteurs**. Because of ninjas' stealthy skills, some people thought they had magical powers. But their success actually relied on science. Ninjas knew how to be stealthy by staying quiet and using **camouflage** effectively. Their weapons required knowledge of certain materials and how they worked in different conditions. Ninjas also had basic knowledge of chemistry and biology to succeed in their secret missions. With the help of science, ninjas became some of history's most effective spies.

Ninjas were deadly assassins. They could quickly strike and kill a target from the shadows and get away without being seen.

FACT

Ninjutsu is the name for the self-defense tactics and philosophy of the ninja. It includes martial arts, combat, spying and sabotage techniques. It also includes spiritual and mental training.

assassin a person secretly hired to kill someone

saboteur a person who purposely damages or destroys property to hinder an enemy

camouflage colouring or covering used to make people or objects look like their surroundings

CHAPTER ONE

WHAT NINJAS REALLY WORE

In movies and TV shows, ninjas are usually shown wearing hooded black outfits. Ninjas did sometimes wear black clothing for stealthy missions. But they also used different types of outfits to hide their identities and help protect them during a fight.

Using camouflage

Ninjas sometimes seemed to have the ability to become invisible. To achieve this, they often wore special camouflage clothing. It hid the outline of their bodies and helped them to blend in with their surroundings. It tricked an enemy's eyes, who saw the ninjas as simply part of the environment.

FACT Black clothing was sometimes dyed with a reddish colour to help hide bloodstains.

Ninjas sometimes used black clothing as camouflage for night-time missions. But they more often wore dark blue or brown clothing. Black clothing tends to outline a person's body, even in the dark. Dark blue blended in better with the colour of the night sky, making it especially difficult to spot the fighter. Sometimes ninjas wore reversible clothing with different colours on each side. They could choose which side to use depending on their surroundings.

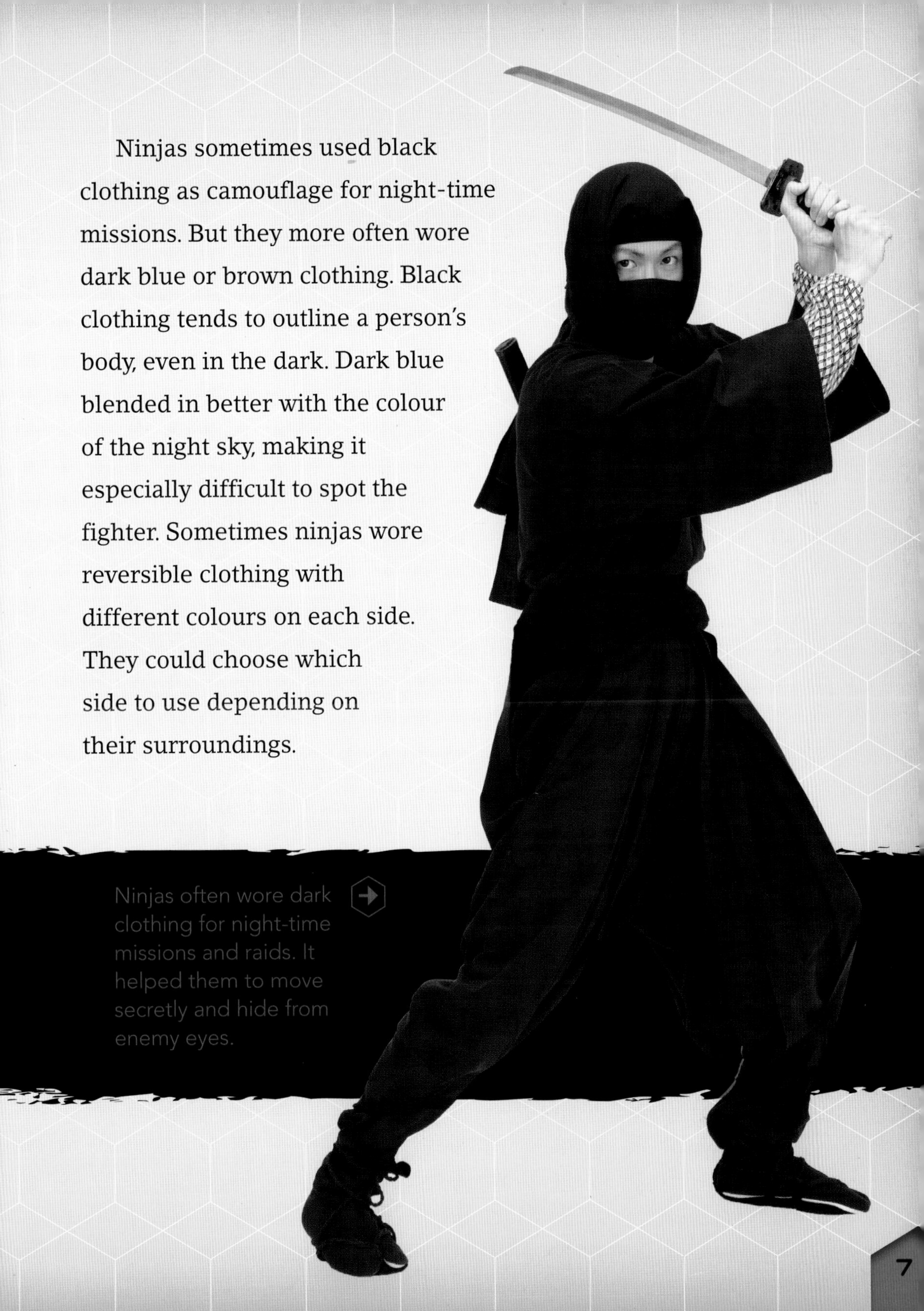

Ninjas often wore dark clothing for night-time missions and raids. It helped them to move secretly and hide from enemy eyes.

Specialized clothing

In addition to helping ninjas hide in the dark, their clothing had various other special uses. Their clothes had many secret pockets used for hiding weapons and other objects. These pockets were designed to let ninjas easily grab and use the equipment they needed.

A tenugui was useful for hiding a ninja's face. But it could also be tied to his sash and used as rope to help climb walls.

Along with their dark clothing, a ninja sometimes wore a cowl or scarf over his face and a hood over his head. These items helped conceal the warrior by hiding the lighter skin of his face. Ninjas often wore *tenugui* to cover their faces. These pieces of cotton cloth had other uses as well. They could be used as belts or as rope to help with climbing.

FACT

Ninjas could use jika-tabi boots to walk in a way that left footprints similar to those of a small child. This made the spies difficult to track.

Fighting footwear

Ninjas often wore *jika-tabi* while on a mission. These boots had soft soles and a split between the big toe and other toes. The soft soles helped a ninja's feet grip various surfaces better. The split toe design mimicked the shape of the human foot, which made the boots more flexible. Together these features helped ninjas quickly and easily climb ropes or walls to achieve their missions.

modern jika-tabi have rubber soles

Armoured protection

Ninjas didn't fight in large battles. They didn't need to use heavy armour. Their clothing was mostly used to conceal them during secret missions. However, ninjas sometimes wore **chain mail** armour called *kusari*. These armoured shirts were lightweight and flexible, yet strong enough to protect ninjas against enemy knives or arrows. Small plates of metal armour called *karuta* could also be sewn into layers of cloth. This light armour helped **disperse** the energy of a weapon blow to keep the warrior's body from absorbing it.

Ninjas could conceal kusari chain mail under normal clothing. The warriors were protected without giving up their secret identity.

HIDDEN IN PLAIN SIGHT

Ninjas saved their dark camouflage for secret night-time missions. Their dark clothing would be too noticeable during the day. For daytime missions, ninjas were experts at hiding in plain sight. They often disguised themselves as ordinary people like farmers or monks. These disguises often helped ninjas to get close to enemies and spy on them more easily.

chain mail a kind of armour made of thousands of iron rings linked together

disperse to spread out over a wide area

CHAPTER TWO

WEAPONS AND GEAR

Ninjas didn't rely only on stealth. They used a variety of deadly weapons as well. But it was the science behind their weapons that helped them succeed in their missions.

Swords and shuriken

Ninjas sometimes used short swords during their missions. These weapons were used more for stabbing attacks than cutting or slicing. The short blades focused the **force** of a ninja's thrusts to pierce an enemy's body. The short length also made the swords quick to draw. Longer swords could restrict a ninja's movements and took longer to draw. These factors took away a ninja's speed advantage in a fight.

Ninjas were perhaps best known for their *shuriken*. Sometimes known as throwing stars, these small, sharp objects could be quickly thrown to damage an enemy. Ninjas held and threw stars by one edge so they would spin through the air. The spinning motion helped shuriken stay stable as they flew. This stability helped ninjas **accurately** hit targets up to 9 metres (30 feet) away. The spinning motion also caused the shuriken to slice deeply into an enemy's flesh.

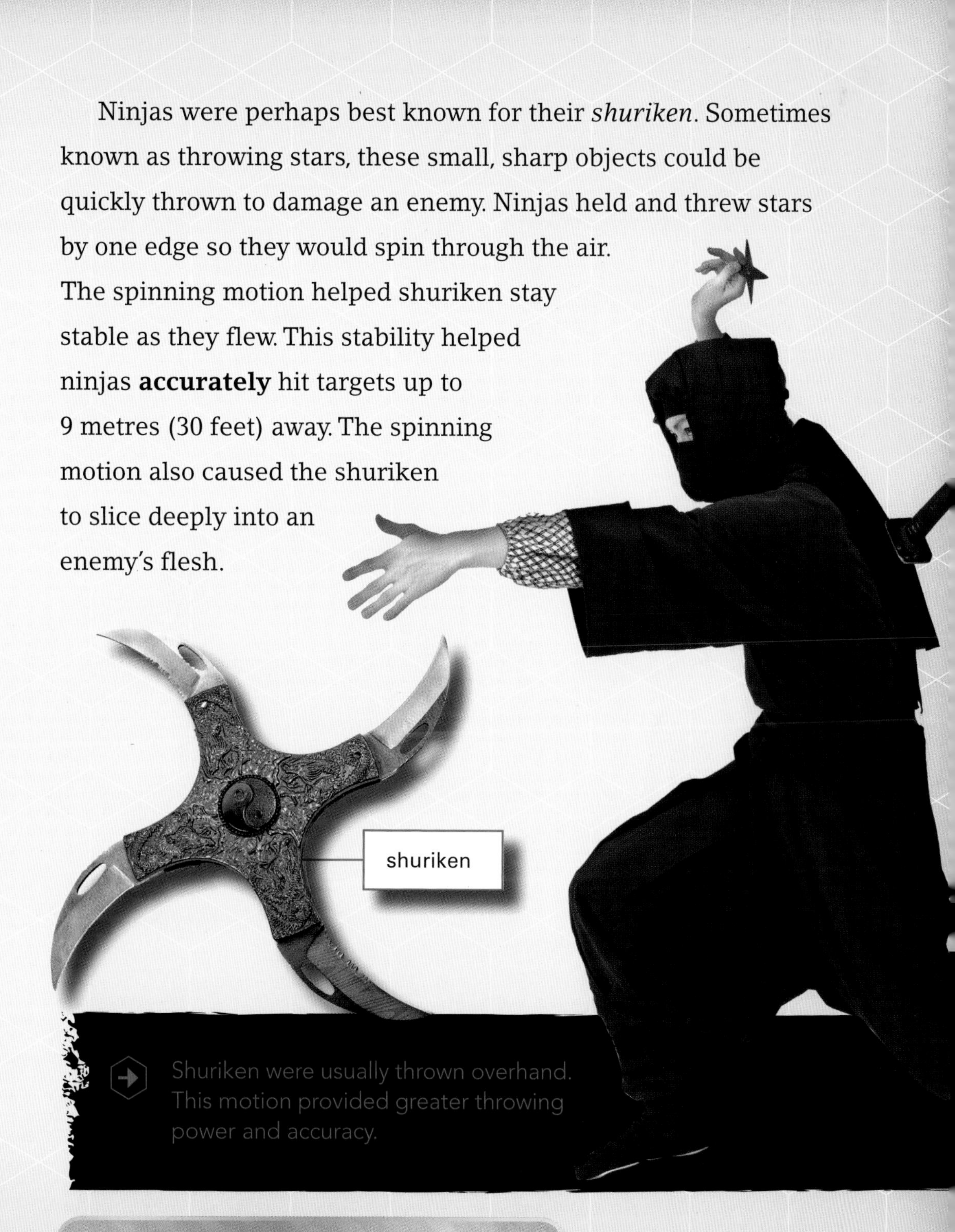

Shuriken were usually thrown overhand. This motion provided greater throwing power and accuracy.

force energy or strength

accurate able to hit a target

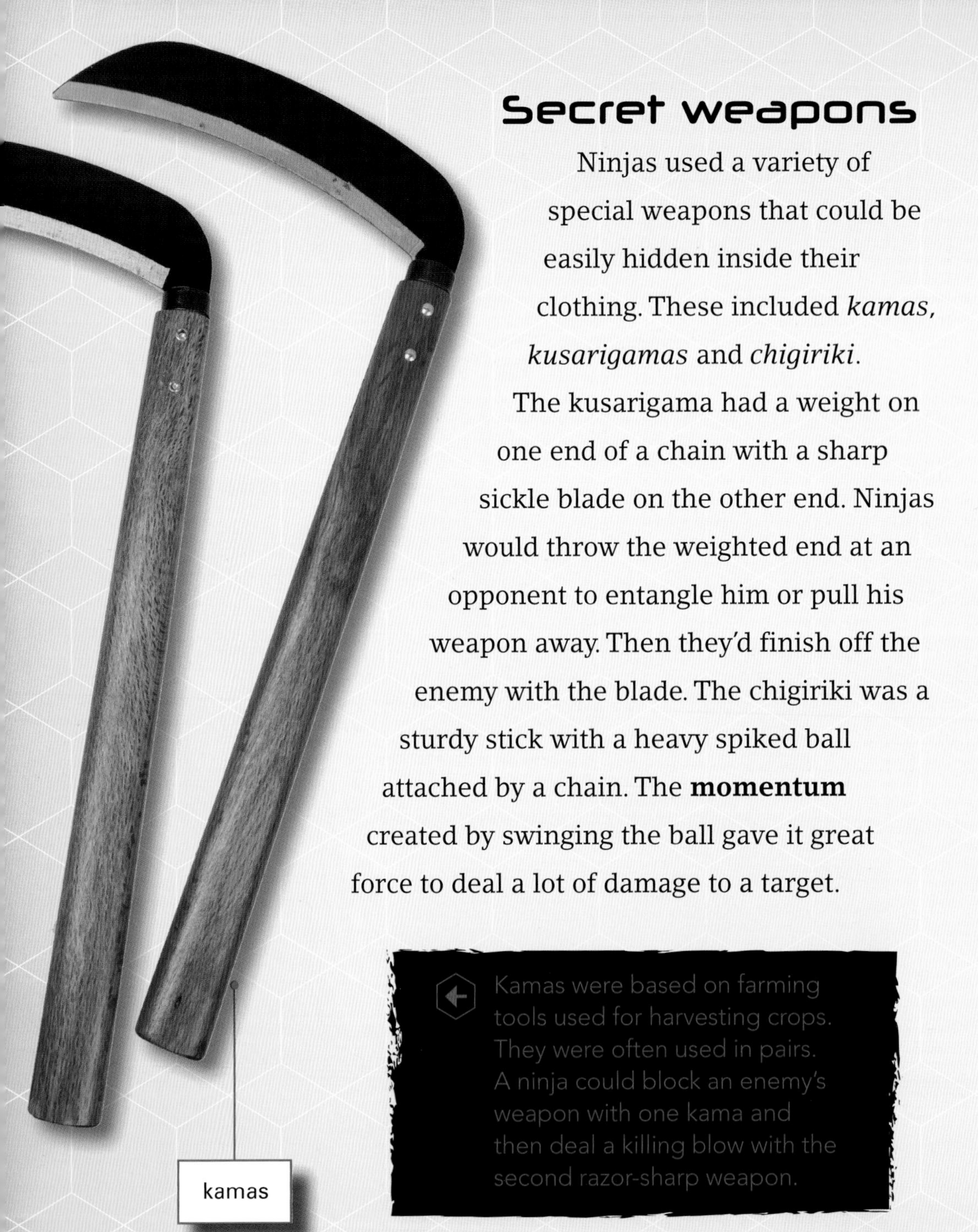

Secret weapons

Ninjas used a variety of special weapons that could be easily hidden inside their clothing. These included *kamas, kusarigamas* and *chigiriki*. The kusarigama had a weight on one end of a chain with a sharp sickle blade on the other end. Ninjas would throw the weighted end at an opponent to entangle him or pull his weapon away. Then they'd finish off the enemy with the blade. The chigiriki was a sturdy stick with a heavy spiked ball attached by a chain. The **momentum** created by swinging the ball gave it great force to deal a lot of damage to a target.

Kamas were based on farming tools used for harvesting crops. They were often used in pairs. A ninja could block an enemy's weapon with one kama and then deal a killing blow with the second razor-sharp weapon.

momentum amount of force in a moving object determined by the object's mass and speed

FACT

Many modern martial arts movies show ninjas fighting with *nunchaku,* or nunchuks. But there is little evidence to show that ninjas ever used these weapons.

Poison weapons

Poison was one of a ninja's most effective hidden weapons. It could be concealed inside a ninja's ring and secretly added to a victim's food or drinks. Some ninja rings had a small point or hook that was coated in poison. If a ninja was discovered, he could stick opponents with the point and the poison would disable them very quickly. Some ninjas even carried blowguns disguised as flutes. A ninja could pose as a musician to get close to his target. Then he could use the blowgun to shoot a victim with a poison dart before sneaking away in the crowd.

Ahead of their time

Ninjas often used equipment that seemed far ahead of its time. For example, police today sometimes use spiked objects called caltrops to puncture the tires of speeding cars. Ninjas used similar objects to stop enemies from pursuing them. They scattered the spiked caltrops on the ground as they made their escape. As enemies stepped on the caltrops, the sharp spikes drove through their soft shoes and into their feet.

Smoke bombs could distract enemies and hide a ninja's movements as he escaped into the night.

CROSSING THE WATER

Fortresses in Japan were often protected by **moats**. To cross them, ninjas swam underwater while breathing through hollow tubes, similar to modern snorkels. Some people think that ninjas may have also used special shoes called *mizugumo*. These devices were made of circular wooden boards that could have allowed ninjas to float by water **displacement**. However, there is little historical evidence to show that ninjas used these special shoes to cross moats.

Ninjas also used weapons similar to modern grenades and smoke bombs. They filled hollow eggs with metal dust or sand. When necessary, they threw these crude grenades at their enemies. When an egg broke, its contents blinded an opponent long enough for a ninja to get away. Smoke bombs were filled with gunpowder and other chemicals. If a ninja had to make a quick escape, a smoke bomb could create a loud noise and a cloud of smoke that hid his movements.

moat deep, wide ditch dug around a castle or fort and filled with water to prevent attacks

displacement movement of something from its position to be replaced by something else; a floating object displaces the volume of a fluid equal to its own

CHAPTER THREE

TRAINING AND FIGHTING TECHNIQUES

Ninjas made good use of their equipment and weapons in their missions. But their greatest advantage was their training. These stealthy warriors constantly worked to strengthen their bodies and sharpen their fighting skills.

Training body and mind

Becoming a ninja required extensive training. Ninjas began physical training as children. They practised to improve their balance and **coordination**. They also trained to strengthen their muscles and become **flexible** to move quickly and quietly.

coordination ability to control body movements

flexible able to bend or move easily

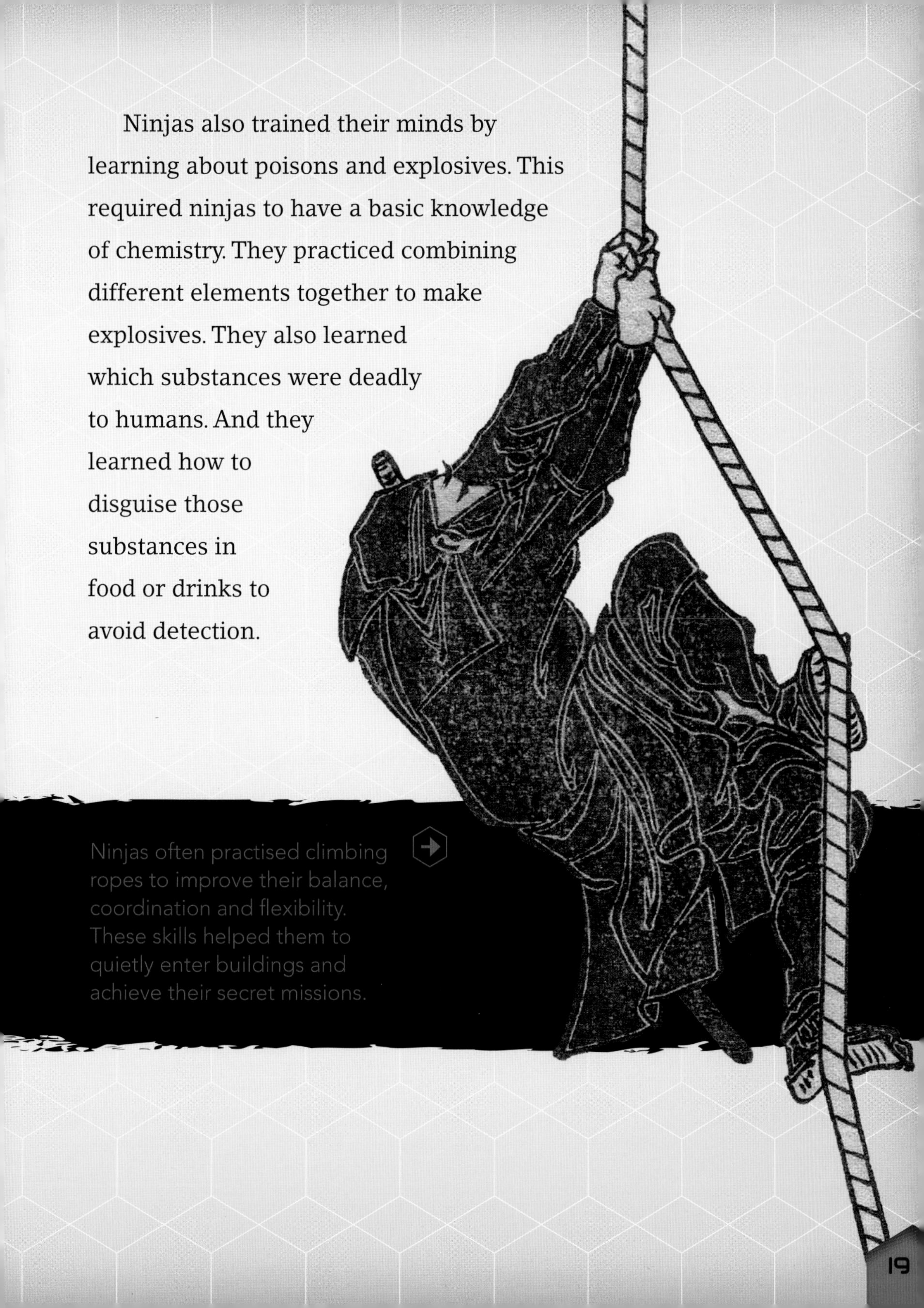

Ninjas also trained their minds by learning about poisons and explosives. This required ninjas to have a basic knowledge of chemistry. They practiced combining different elements together to make explosives. They also learned which substances were deadly to humans. And they learned how to disguise those substances in food or drinks to avoid detection.

Ninjas often practised climbing ropes to improve their balance, coordination and flexibility. These skills helped them to quietly enter buildings and achieve their secret missions.

Ninjas learned to walk and move in total silence to avoid being discovered during their stealthy missions. They practised several techniques for many long hours to master these skills.

Becoming "invisible"

Hundreds of years ago many people thought ninjas could become invisible. However, ninjas had simply mastered the ability to conceal themselves. They wore camouflage clothing and learned how to be totally silent and still. In this way, they blended into their surroundings and could be nearly impossible to see.

When ninjas did move, they did it slowly and smoothly. Quick, jerky movements could attract attention. Ninjas learned to move based on their surroundings. They avoided creating **silhouettes** that could be seen by enemies.

Silent movement

Ninjas used a special method to learn to move in nearly perfect silence. They practised walking on ice while wearing wooden sandals. This helped them develop excellent balance while stepping carefully to avoid making noise on the ice.

While on missions, ninjas usually wore specially cushioned sandals that helped absorb noise. They also used a special walk called the *shinobi-ashi* to move silently. The little toe of the foot was placed on the ground first. Then the warrior's weight was shifted to the big toe. This technique prevented the noise of an entire foot hitting the ground at once.

silhouette outline of something that shows its shape

More ninja techniques

Ninja warriors didn't normally fight in large battles in the open. Their missions took place in stealth and secrecy. They usually worked alone. However, they did need to work as a team occasionally.

Sometimes one ninja would hold another on his shoulders to help him reach a window. Other times these two ninjas would give a third warrior a helpful boost to fly over a wall. Another technique required four ninjas. Three warriors would create a human pyramid to help the fourth reach a window or other high point. The ninjas on the first level supported the weight of the third warrior. The pyramid was very stable, and allowed the fourth warrior to quickly climb up to the intended location.

Creating stable human pyramids required physical strength and a good sense of balance.

THE FOUR ELEMENTS

Some say that ninja stealth techniques were inspired by four elements of nature: earth, air, fire and water. A fire technique might mean setting a fire to distract guards. An air technique could be to hide in a tree at night dressed in dark colours to blend in with the night sky. One water technique involved spreading duckweed on the surface of a pond or river. The duckweed helped hide a warrior as he swam beneath it. Earth techniques included curling into a motionless ball to appear like a stone or other part of the landscape. All of these techniques required ninjas to train to become observant and familiar with nature.

CHAPTER FOUR

NINJAS IN ACTION

Ninjas were successful warriors because of their stealth and intelligence. But they were also very good at **psychological** warfare. They used tactics like fear, propaganda and threats to reduce an enemy's **morale**.

Psychological weapons

Ninjas used several psychological tricks to make enemies afraid and distrustful of one another. They disguised themselves by wearing the same clothing as their enemies. This helped them easily enter an enemy stronghold to cause confusion and distraction.

Ninjas were also skilled at using fire to sabotage an enemy's defenses. However, they didn't just set fire inside an enemy's castle. They instead set fires in ways to appear as if traitors in the enemy's own army did it. These actions often caused enemies to worry more about their own men than their ninja opponents.

psychological relating to the mind

morale feelings or state of mind of a person or group of people

Ninjas used psychology to their advantage during missions. They knew how to frighten and confuse their enemies to avoid being caught or killed.

Kuji-kiri were special signs made with the fingers. These hand movements were used as a form of psychological warfare. Many people thought a ninja could use kuji-kiri to place a magical curse on them.

Ninjas sometimes kidnapped people in the middle of the night. They could make it appear as if a victim simply vanished. This created great fear and strengthened people's beliefs that ninjas had supernatural abilities.

NINJA WARNING SYSTEMS

People feared ninjas so much they created ways to warn themselves if the assassins were near. Buildings were designed with hidden trip wires that rang alarm bells. Walkways were made with crunchy gravel, and floors were built with squeaky boards. People hoped to hear an approaching ninja and escape before he could strike.

Fearing the supernatural

Ninjas were excellent at using fire, explosives, poison and camouflage to create distraction and fear. They were also very skilled at observing their enemies. They could determine an enemy's strengths and weaknesses and used this knowledge to their advantage.

Sometimes ninjas would kill an enemy and leave the body for others to find. But they were careful not to leave any marks on the body or other clues about how the person died. This added to the ninjas' **reputation** as frightening supernatural beings. Ninjas encouraged this fear by staying secret and hidden. They knew their reputation made them more frightening, which helped them be more successful in their missions.

reputation a person's character, as judged by other people

Success with science

Ninjas were highly skilled and greatly feared. But the secret to their success was based in science. Physical science helped them train their bodies to be strong and nimble. The science behind their weapons and equipment helped ninjas be stealthy fighters and spies. Ninjas even used the science of the mind. They knew how to strike fear into their enemies and defeat them without any combat at all. Ninjas relied on science in almost everything they did to succeed in their missions.

From weapons and gear to psychological warfare, science helped ninjas become some of the most feared and successful warriors of history.

NINJA TECHNIQUES LIVE ON

Ninja teachings and skills are similar to skills used in today's military. Special Forces soldiers move silently and use camouflage during their missions. Special Forces also use martial arts skills in hand-to-hand combat, such as blocking, punching, kicking and using pressure points.

GLOSSARY

accurate able to hit a target

assassin a person secretly hired to kill someone

camouflage colouring or covering used to make people or objects look like their surroundings

chain mail kind of armour made of thousands of iron rings linked together

coordination ability to control body movements

disperse to spread out over a wide area

displacement movement of something from its position to be replaced by something else; a floating object displaces the volume of a fluid equal to its own

flexible able to bend or move easily

force energy or strength

moat deep, wide ditch dug around a castle or fort and filled with water to prevent attacks

momentum amount of force in a moving object determined by the object's mass and speed

morale feelings or state of mind of a person or group of people

psychological relating to the mind

reputation a person's character, as judged by other people

saboteur a person who purposely damages or destroys property to hinder an enemy

silhouette outline of something that shows its shape

Comprehension questions

1. Many people thought that ninjas had magical powers. What specific things did ninjas do that made people think this?
2. Imagine yourself as a modern ninja warrior. What skills would you need to learn to avoid being seen or heard by your enemies?

Books

Avoid Being a Ninja Warrior (The Danger Zone), John Malam (Book House, 2012)

Ninja-rella (Far Out Fairy Tales), Joey Comeau (Raintree, 2016)

Ninjas and Samurai: A Nonfiction Companion to Magic Tree House #5: Night of the Ninjas (Magic Tree House Fact Tracker), Mary Pope Osborne and Natalie Pope Boyce (Random House, 2014)

Websites

www.funkidslive.com/video/learn-ninja-moves
Watch a video about children learning ninja moves and be inspired to learn some yourself!

www.youngsamurai.com/site/YOUN/Templates/General.aspx?pageid=5&cc=GB
Learn more about weapons, the art of zen and the difference between ninja and samurai.

web-japan.org/kidsweb/travel/ninja/ninja01.html
Learn about ninja and the art of ninjutsu on this website.